AF261339

What Can Alexa Do?

<u>What Is Alexa?</u>

Alexa is a cloud based virtual assistant similar to Siri or OK Google. Have I lost you already? Don't worry. I'll talk you through it.

Alexa is cloud based, meaning it doesn't exist in your devices or on hardware within your home, on your wrist, in your car or anywhere else you care to imagine. It is a program that sits on a remote (meaning "not around here") server. A server is just a computer that serves – or does stuff for you. Okay, so it's a program that someone put on a computer somewhere, connected to the internet and it does stuff. Yes, it's artificially intelligent, but what does that mean for you?

Well, it's got a whole load of cool things it can do from speech to text, text to speech, working out your voice pattern and the difference between your voice and your partner's voice, setting timers, alarms, playing songs and linking to hundreds of different services to provide a very rich environment for entertainment, security, information, tutelage and smart home automation. We'll get to all that.

In the meantime, we need to know the difference between what Alexa is and what things like the Amazon Echo Dots are. The Echo dots have Alexa built into them, but they are NOT Alexa. It's a bit like saying that cars are the fuel, a sandwich is cheese or a TV is a TV programme. Each contains the things within but are not defined by them. If we take my previous analogy of a TV not being a programme, this is probably the closest analogy I can think of. The echo dot, echo show or any other "thing" with Alexa in it can do lots of "stuff", but if you unplug it, Alexa is no longer inside it. It's not that she just needs power… she's actually not there. The echo or echo dot is the physical thing that has the link to the internet. We link to the Alexa service using the internet (wifi) and your own amazon account. We can get onto how to link to it all in a jiffy, but the key thing to remember here is the difference between the hardware and the software.

The software exists on the cloud, away from your home and you access that using the hardware inside your home. That's why you may get the red ring and the horrible "bongggggggg" sound before it tells you that the connection to the internet is poor. Alexa will not do anything during these moments, because it can't. Interestingly, when these errors sound, the device (hardware) itself… the physical thing… is what's telling you about the lack of the connection. It's not Alexa that does that. Confused yet?

Well, Amazon want you to think that Alexa is an omnipresent virtual assistant and so they try to blur the lines and hide what's actually happening.

What they want you to think is that Alexa sits in your living room (or wherever), waiting to help you. What's actually happening is that the device sits in your house, and connects using wifi to a service that they hold on their servers. Your device communicates at the speed of light with the service that they hold in their server room (probably in America). When there's an error and it can't connect, your hardware has a VERY limited functionality that recognises you saying the "wake word" (we'll get on to that in a second) and it says "nope, I can't connect"… in other words, obviously.

So what the [little black dot] is a "wake word"?

The devices with Alexa built in need to do one thing and one thing only. They need to recognise when you say the "wake word", then they need to send data up to the Alexa server and return the result. Everything else is done by the Alexa server. So – to a large extent – don't worry about what the Alexa server does – at least don't worry about it for now… we can get to more complex stuff later in this book.

In other words, the device needs to be able to recognise when you say "Alexa" or whatever wake word you choose. By default, you can use the word "Alexa", "computer" (like in star trek), "echo" or "Amazon". I've actually seen a great little hack where you can actually "jail break" this functionality so you can set your own wake word, but I'm not going to get into that here.

So a wake word simply wakes up the device so it starts listening to whatever follows it.
It works like this:

The device is CONSTANTLY listening for a voice pattern that matches its wake-word criteria. These criteria are hard coded into the device so it doesn't need a wifi signal to know you're calling it. Once it "hears" the wake word (in all examples to follow, our wake word is "Alexa"), it starts "recording". I put the word "recording" in inverted commas because it doesn't keep that recording. All it does it take it, transcribe it into text and then sends it to the Alexa server. These voice commands could be anything from "turn on the lights" to "what's the weather like in New York?" The Alexa service is very versatile and relies on things called "skills" to make it even more effective. We will get to the skills chapter later on in the book too. Don't worry. I'll stick with you on this.

Alexa is constantly developing and being added to new products. New skills are being added and with great new innovations like IFTTT and Stringify, you're able to really leverage the Alexa service to do some pretty impressive stuff. Routines allow you to stack many things together and operate based on certain conditions.

As an example of some of the things I now do with Alexa (and I'll explain these later), I can send a text message to both my mum, and my dad (who have divorced) to let them know when I get home, but only after a long drive to drop off my kids to their mum. They live 100 miles from me and I see them every two weeks. I can text my wife when I leave work, so she knows I'm coming to pick her up. I can do both of these text-routines without doing anything! I can set the temperature of my house but only do it based on where I am by working out what the traffic is like and how long it will take me to get home, how long it will take the house to warm up and only start the heating at the right time so it gets up to heat by the time I'm home. There are routines I can create in my house so I can change the TV from watching Virgin media to watching the Apple TV, or Firestick to virgin media. If I want to record a show or a series, I can ask Alexa to record it. I can change the colour of my living room using the LED strip lights, I can ask Alexa to send a text message to my stepson when dinner is ready to prevent me having to shout at him. I set routines to remind my wife to take her tablets, wake me up for work, organise my shopping list, listen to audiobooks, control lighting in groups so I can turn on the whole of downstairs. This is particularly useful when I am in my bedroom but need to get a drink from the kitchen by walking through the living room. I can view my security cameras both on my phone and in the kitchen using the echo show. I can check if the lights are on from anywhere in the world, work out how long it will take me to get to work and get the latest headlines emailed to my work inbox. I can use my phone as a DAB digital radio in my car… the things you can do with Alexa are endless and needless to say… I love it. So let's start by dispelling some myths and work out what Alexa is NOT.

<u>What Alexa Is Not</u>

Why is it that Alexa seems so controversial? I bought an echo dot third generation for my Dad – he's very much a techie and started using computers way back in the 1980s as a CAD (computer aided design) system for his architecture practice before most people even knew what CAD was. I started programming on an Atari in 1988 (when I was 8) and started lecturing in computer game design when I was 10, so I'm pretty techie myself but I definitely got it from him. And yet, my dear old dad asked me to take the gift back – thinking he'd never use it because he was worried about the security implications. I'll get on to the security issues later in the chapter entitled "is it dangerous", but for now, I wanted to focus on what Alexa is NOT. We've already discussed that Alexa is stored in the cloud, and what that means. This implies that Alexa is not a hardware thing that sits on your table right? Exactly! Alexa is not a thing you buy. You buy access to it in the same way as a season pass allows you access to football matches, or a membership of a club allows you access to cheap drinks. Alexa is not hardware. I hope that's clear.

What else is it not? It's not anything more or less than an engine. Alexa allows you to access content by linking stuff together. In a similar way to the world wide web being a way of connecting web pages together so you can view them, and the internet connect stuff together so you can move from site to site, send emails from one person to another, the Alexa service allows you to connect your hardware to other stuff. It's part of the "internet of things" or "web 3.0". these are potentially scary terms, which (in my opinion) aim to alienate normal people. I remember going to the internet marketing show where there was a huge buzz about "web 2.0".

What was this mythical new technology?

It was pretty boring to be honest. After thinking this was a massively high-tech development in computer technology, I eventually plucked up the courage to ask someone who explained it was nothing more or less than people being able to interact with web pages beyond the simple "click this link" stuff. Web 2.0 was a way of describing the next stage of the internet, where people could log in, customise designs of pages, or content, specifically for the person who's viewing it. Nowadays, it's standard. To be frank, I remember adding this kind of functionality about 7 years before the show in which people were telling me it was "new".

Web 3.0 on the other hand is the next development in web technology and it's basically the "internet of things". ARGH there's that phrase again! Calm down… it's simply that things can now connect to wifi to do stuff. The internet is not just a web browser and a web page. The internet includes email, smart home stuff and – yes – Alexa. The internet of things is simply the Alexa kind of stuff… smart home stuff. The internet of things is literally that… stuff that connects to the internet and makes changes in the world based on something that happens online. More often than not, it's boring… something like a light switch turning on. It's most basic command might be you clicking a button on an app and a light going on or off. That's the real-world "thing" changing its nature in response to something that happens on the internet (the button press). Of course it can be a LOT more complex than that too.
Okay, so is Alexa the internet of things?

No. But it does work in that space. It serves the internet of things in the same way as any other virtual assistant. Is it essential? No. But it does make things a lot easier. There are many things that Alexa is not. It is not the oracle we have all been waiting for. It is not going to solve all of your problems. It is not the singularity (see "is it dangerous" later). It will make your life easier if you use it right, it might save you money in the long-term but likely cost quite a lot in the short term – depending on how deeply you go into it. It is currently (at the time of writing) the most popular voice assistant with the most compatibility of all of them and it works most of the time. It has a few minor issues which I will discuss later, but in general, I'm a big fan so let's get into the nitty gritty to explain why, but first, let's address those security concerns, shall we?

Is Alexa Dangerous?

In his book, Superintelligence, author, Nick Bostrom explains how artificially intelligent machines could gain sentience. It's terrifying… not just in the almost-inaccessible way it's written (long words, you know), but also in the picture he paints of the horrific fate that could befall the human race as a result of the emergence of artificial intelligence. Now, I admit that the following analogy if a bit woolly – or furry, to be exact, but in 1998, I wrote an article called "Don't fear Furbies". There was a massive hype about these furry little toys being able to talk to one another in a coded language called Furbish. In the article, I explained Isaac Asimov's three laws of robotics:

- A robot may not injure a human being or, through inaction, allow a human being to come to harm.
- A robot must obey orders given it by human beings except where such orders would conflict with the First Law.
- A robot must protect its own existence as long as such protection does not conflict with the First or Second Law.

Using these laws, we can control robots. Having said that, does Alexa have control over such processes that it would be able to cause harm anyway? Certainly Furbies didn't.

Can you imagine a little pink plastic creature gaining sentience? What would it do with such power? Squeak us into submission? What would happen when the batteries ran flat?

Obviously things have moved on and the emergence of Alexa as a voice assistant has caused another flurry of panic. Interestingly, people tend not to be too worried about the possibility of sentience – which in my opinion is a distinct possibility in the future, but more concerned about people listening in on private conversations and sending spying information to the US government. At the time of writing, more than 100 million Alexa devices have been sold. Let's assume for the sake of argument and easy mathematics that every person who owns one has more than one… let's say 10. They own 10 of them. It's not impossible. It's perhaps unlikely, but let's be conservative. That's 10 million people. Now, let's assume that of those people, half of them are asleep half of the time.

Again, possible. That's 5 million let's say only one fifth of the time, someone is saying something around these devices. That resolves to 1 million conversations at any one time that needs to be monitored. That's a massive undertaking, and (frankly), I don't think the US government could be bothered to listen in. In our house for example, any US government official would be treated to episodes of Coronation Street, a circular saw and hammering from my DIY efforts, and the occasional fire alarm when I burn the dinner. My personal conversations would be boring and of no interest to security services. I recognise that there are many videos online where they ask Alexa if they're being monitored and the device beeps and turns off. But it does that if you say a phrase like "I like to eat ice cream with a lot of chocolate sprinkles and toppings including strawberry sauce. My favourite ice cream is mint choc chip". Is it that Alexa thinks people who eat this kind of ice cream are terrorists or is it (more likely) that it just doesn't have an appropriate response programmed for what you said? It's mad to think that just because there is no reply, the device is spying on you.

Let's assume for the sake of argument that I'm wrong, however. Let's assume that yes, the device you paid for is indeed trying to cause personal harm, damage or loss to its customer base – because that's good business practice. What can Alexa or the government do about it?

In the UK, we are covered by GDPR – a strict guidance on the usage of personal data. These restrictions are relaxed a bit in the US, sure, but it's still illegal to spy on people. Let's look at this a little more… we can do a simple text to see if the device is actually using the internet. It's called a modem. Modem stands for modulator-demodulator, and at the risk of getting too techie, it works like this: Data is modulated, or turned into beepy wizzy information chunks and sent down a line. Then the beepy wizzy information chunks get de-modulated and decoded. That's basically it. It's like when you send a letter… your thoughts are written down onto paper, thrown into a box, the paper is sent and at the other end, someone reads the paper to work out what your thoughts are. It's a way of "modulating" your thoughts onto paper, and then de-modulating them back into someone else's head. Same thing with a modem, except it's doing it with a computer's "thoughts". So how do we know a letter has been sent? We see the letter… well, we can also monitor the wifi "line" to see if a wifi signal is being sent when an Alexa device is "dormant" – that is before the wake word is said. Can we see any activity? No. Is there ANY way that Alexa is monitoring you? I don't think so… It's not doing it by wifi, that's for certain. So why are people still worried? Well, there have been stories about Alexa recording a private conversation and sending it to someone. That DID happen. However, although that sounds horrible and invasive, this is what must have happened:

Alexa thinks it heard the wake word. It then wakes up. It then thinks it hears the command to send a message. It asks who to send it to. The humans in the room ignore the device and keep chatting. Alexa thinks it recognises the name and repeats it back to check it got the right person. The humans ignore it again and carry on talking. The Alexa device thinks it hears "yes" and then says something like "what's the message?". The humans then ignore it again and keep talking while Alexa records the conversation. Alexa then says "got it. Shall I send it now?". The humans ignore it again and keep talking. Alexa thinks it hears "yes" again and sends it to someone who already exists on the contact list. This is not a case of sending the message to a random person or the CIA – this is someone the device owner knows.
Sounds unlikely? Of course, but 100 million devices (see above) recording 24-7, this kind of thing will eventually happen. It's the law of certainty. With that amount of information, it's certain to happen eventually. But I blame the humans for ignoring the Alexa prompts. They could have said "nevermind" at ANY point to stop the message being sent.

Let's assume I'm wrong. All of my IT knowledge is worthless, my first class IT degree is fake and I'm making all of this up. What can the risks be? Perhaps Amazon would like to hear about your day at work or how much seasoning your lunch needs, but it's unlikely. The sheer resources to monitor this amount of data is increasing daily and they would soon be victims of their own success if they had to monitor everyone. If Alexa does provide any weak spot, however, it is that if someone managed to hack in to your home, they could turn your heating up, control your lights or play music in your house. That's not too bad. Potentially a smart lock could be a worry, but I don't think I'd want to link that to Alexa. Keep your passwords safe, but in my opinion the risk is very minimal anyway and I wouldn't want a smart lock that could be unlocked remotely just in case something went wrong with it.

To conclude… is Alexa dangerous? No. Don't be stupid.

A Bit About Apps

We need to begin our journey by explaining what apps are, how they work and why it's so important to use apps with Alexa to extend the range of things Alexa can do.

Apps (or "applications") are little programs that get installed on phones, tablets, even computers nowadays. Each Alexa enabled device tends to have its own app. Each device links to the service that makes that device work and requires you to set up an account. It's the app that allows you to log in to your account. Once you're logged in, you can do stuff within your account to link your devices and get them to do stuff. Have a look at the infrared chapter for the most comprehensive guide to doing thinks in an app but for now we must be content with knowing that apps allow us to link to our devices. Once we have done that we need to enable the skill within the Alexa app.

The Alexa app is the place where you are able to link all of your devices to the Alexa service using skills. See the skills chapter for more information on skills.

The main problem with everything having their own app is that your phone or tablet can get a bit overloaded with them if there are too many of them. Thankfully, once you've added the functionality you want, it's usually possible to delete them from your device until you need to make hangers again. If you don't delete them, they can get a bit prolific.

Adding Some Skills

Skills, on the other hand, are very useful and since it's all held on Amazon's services, you don't really have a limit on how many you can enable. The only issue is when Alexa thinks it's heard something that you didn't intend and she gets a bit jumpy. She likes to be helpful and I discovered recently that if you fart next to Alexa, after saying the wake word, she starts playing the poo poo song on Spotify. Coincidence? Maybe.
Skills allow Alexa to link to third party servers and it's usually what allows smart home devices to work with her. It's great because most of them are free. You will need to pay for some functionality - especially when this is linked to hardware or games, but on the whole, they don't cost anything.

The rule of thumb is that if there's something a skill can do, just enable it. You may need a good memory if you enable too many because some have very odd launch phrases. There's even one where you can talk to Alexa in cat language by meowing at it and it'll meow back. Mental!

Things With Alexa In It

You might be surprised to hear that it's not just stuff that amazon make that has Alexa built into it. Amazon are nice people and they've decided to open their brains to other third party systems that can add the Alexa service to their proprietary devices.

Oooh now the good stuff. There are loads of things out there with Alexa built into it and the great thing (in my opinion) is that Amazon are allowing third party developers access to the Alexa platform. Anything with a skill can be Alexa compatible (see "skills" later in this book), but there's a difference between being Alexa compatible and having Alexa built in.

Strictly speaking, Alexa is not going to be built in to anything, but rather it will have the ability to access the service. For the purpose of this chapter, we'll assume they're the same thing. Those items with Alexa built in include all the stuff that comes from Amazon itself. The Amazon-branded products include the Echo, Echo Plus, Echo Dot, Echo Spot, Echo Show, Echo Input, some remotes, the Firestick (Fire TV), some of the newer Kindle Fires and even the Fire Phone, which they stopped making after disappointing sales figures. Does that surprise you?

It's more than just this list, however. There are a growing number of other devices with Alexa built in. For example, the Roav Viva from Anker is a car charger (two USB ports) that links via Bluetooth to a mobile phone. Using this service, and via the Roav Viva App, Alexa functionality can control your phone, call people on your contact list, work out the time it will take to get places (it works out where you're most likely to be going) and you can even turn your phone into a DAB digital radio by asking for a radio station from TuneIn (a radio service compatible with Alexa).

There are SatNavs with Alexa built in, smart speakers like the Anker Eufy Genie, alarm clocks like iHome iAV2, (which doesn't technically have Alexa built in, but it will as soon as you put your echo dot inside it), and even showers that can enable Alexa capabilities through the water spout!

The Roav Viva works really well if you have Bluetooth enabled on your phone and it even allows you to link via your phone to the car's Bluetooth too. I use it all the time to listen to audiobooks, make calls and listen to the radio, hands-free. I can use it to work out the traffic to my destination, give me directions to the nearest petrol station, fast food drive thru, get film times if I'm stuck in traffic on my way to the cinema, and it also does all the stuff you'd expect from Alexa. I used it to control my Christmas lights when I forgot to turn them off in the morning, when I left the house early. Yes, it's geeky, but that's why we love it.

Regarding things that are compatible with our dear virtual friend, we have a gazillion things to pick from.
If it's a security camera and you do or think you might want to have it Alexa enabled, you're in luck. Most things are, nowadays and while you may pay a tiny bit more for the functionality, you're very likely to find something within your budget. For example, I have two Netvue Orb Cams. They're versatile, you can even mount them on the ceiling and invert the picture in the app. I can then view them using my phone on their own Netvue app, or on my Echo Show.

I'm able to talk through the speaker in the camera itself, and hear the responses. This camera has been REALLY helpful after my wife had an epileptic seizure. I logged in to the camera to check she was okay, and was able to inform my mother-in-law who came around. I even got a notification when she arrived by automating my cameras to notify me when they detected motion.

I have many smart plugs all over the place and these can be useful for turning on and off power to standing lights and light strips as well as my shaver (which needs charging every day, ideally), a fan (which can be turned on automatically if it gets too hot) and even an oven to turn on and pre-heat before I get home. Note that this could be a fire hazard, so maybe be careful about this kind of thing. We can also use wemo switches which get wired directly into any device so as to turn ANYTHING into a smart-switched electrical thing. The possibilities with smart switches are amazing.

I've even added a smart switch to something that (technically) didn't need it. I'll cover this more in the chapter entitled Infra-red, but I added a smart switch to my light strip in my living room. The reason for this is that I wanted Alexa to know when my living room light strip is on. If I'm only using infra-red, I'm not going to know, because the on and off command are the same, so instead of using infra-red for that command, I just use the smart switch to turn it on and off. This status can then be checked using Alexa because the smart switch maintains just enough power to report if the socket is on or off. This is really useful if I'm out and want to know if the light strip was left on. If it was, I can get a text message saying what has been left on.

Very handy for saving money. Certain plugs also give access to energy usage graphs and charts that can help you track your spending and energy consumption.

Next is my Broadlink RM3 Mini. This thing is affectionately known as the "Black Bean" and it controls infra-red devices like my TV. I won't go into it in too much detail right now, but I cover this in greater depth in the chapter called Infra-red. It has its pros and cons as I'll discuss later.

Lastly (for my house, anyway), is the Nest 3rd generation learning thermostat. As the name suggests, this thermostat works out what the pattern is for my heating and it works out what to do with that information. Right now, for example, I'm at work, writing this, but I've just checked the temperature in my house. It's 13 degrees C.

That's chilly.

We don't have any pets, and everyone is out so it's not the end of the world, but if I want that hotter (and I do, when I get home), it can work out how long I will take to get home and how long it'll take to get up to temperature and start heating up while I'm on my way. Clever! It also tells me how many hours of heating I have used and gives me points (called "Leaves") when I turn the heating off and use less energy. I can use it with IFTTT (more on that later) and Stringify (more on that later, too) to really hyper-charge the usefulness of the internet of things!

Alexa Lights

Lights are possibly the first thing you're going to want to get your hands on, when starting to play with Alexa. It's the first thing I did, anyway. My wife bought me an echo dot for Christmas 2017 and since then, our home has been totally transformed. We now have smart switches in the bedroom for two little side-lights as well as under-cabinet lights in the kitchen, a standing light in the living room and a colour changing, dimmable light strip around the ceiling to provide mood lighting in the living room. Now, I've got a few things going on here, and there are a few options available to you too so be aware of this. The first kind of light I got was a colour changing light bulb.

These can be very good, but can also be a bit of a problem. I'm not really sure what happened to mine, but I suspect that using it in the kitchen might have been a bit too much humidity for it. I suspect something shorted because it will no-longer work and so I threw it out. It wasn't particularly expensive – it was from Lombex and probably cost about £20. The problem is when you have a lot of them to replace at the same time.

I've been told by a friend of mine that IKEA are now selling smart lights and he used LED dimmable spot lights (formerly halogens) but they're £7 each – not bad pricing… except when you need to replace 12 of them to get the right effect. Something else you need to bear in mind here is that LEDs are the best way to go because they are low wattage and last longer, but they are more expensive and if they're on the same circuit as non-LED bulbs, they're likely to receive more power than they need, causing them to burn out first, before the cheaper, but higher-power bulbs. In other words, if you're going to replace any bulbs at all, replace all of them in one go!

Okay, so that's smart bulbs. Great idea, but can be expensive. The other thing is that they sometimes need a hub. Certainly, the Phillips Hue bulbs (expensive, reliable and very popular) do. The good news is that some of the Alexa devices also have a hub built in, nowadays. I bought an Echo Show 2nd generation for my son for Christmas. I was worried when the free bulb turned out to be a Phillips hue because I knew it needed a hub. The good thing was though that the Echo Show 2nd Generation (unlike the first generation) has a built-in hub, so connecting the bulb was as easy as asking Alexa to discover devices.

Bulbs are good because you can tell them to turn on and off, change colour (depending on whether they allow you to do that or not, obviously) and dim (if they can). The main issue is their fairly short life and high cost and their need for constant power. They need the switch to be turned on in order for them to work by receiving the order from the wifi so it can be very annoying if your spouse has turned off the light switch, only for you to scream at Alexa to turn it on… because it won't ever work until you turn the switch to "on" again.

Right, enough about bulbs for a minute, because I don't use them now anyway.

The next thing is the smart plugs, which I covered a lot in the last video. Using the devices settings in the Alexa App, it's very easy to change a plug into a light. It's a good idea to do this so that you can then control all the lights with a command like "Alexa, lights on". Everything in that room that Alexa knows is a light will then turn on. If you leave it as a plug, that's okay, but you won't be able to say "lights on" unless you call it "lights" and that's just silly.

As I said in the last chapter, I use smart switches for lights to allow me to find out if they're on or off and it can be useful to get this status. For more information on using them in conjunction with a colour changing light strip, check out the chapter called Infra-red.

Okay, so on to my under-cabinet lights. This is perhaps a little cheat, but I soldered my ultra-bright white-only LED light strip to a power supply unit and I plugged it into a smart switch which I keep behind the microwave. I called it "cabinets" and added it to the kitchen "lights" group. I also added it to the "downstairs" group so that it can come on when I say "Alexa, downstairs on". This is a bit of a cheat, because it's actually a smart switch that does the clever bits, but I think it counts. It helps to illustrate that you can mix and match technologies to get the effect you're after. Now, a little tip… I found that the adhesive on LED light strips tends to be pretty poor and certainly not good enough to hold the weight of the power cable. In my under-cabinet light setup, I screwed a tiny hook into the under-side of the cabinet so that it can take the majority of the weight of the cable. Since doing that, I've never had the LED strip lights de-laminate (fall off) from the cabinets.

Finally (in my house, at least) is the colour changing, dimmable LED light strip in the living-room. I chose a system that can easily be expanded by plugging in one strip to the next one in a kind of daisy-chain. We have this in my step-son's room too, but his is dumb as he doesn't like Alexa much. It might be something to do with me setting an alarm to wake him up every morning by calling him a lazy boy, followed by playing a selection of bubble gum pop songs. Oh, I know how to get the kids up!

There are smart switches too, and these can obviously control things like lights, but there's a whole chapter on that and I don't want to spoil the fun.

The light strip in the living room is (technically) dumb, but I've got around that by using the Broadlink RM3 Mini (the Black Bean) and a smart switch. It's an infra-red controlled lightstrip with a cheap and nasty control unit, but I'll get onto the infra-red functionality in a later chapter. For now, let's focus on the "on-off" functionality of the smart switch that I plugged it in to. I use this together with routines to control whether the light is on or off. By adding this to the living room and downstairs groups, I can control it by saying "Alexa, light on" while in the living room" or "Alexa, living room on" (which also turns on the TV) and "Alexa, downstairs on" which turns on the lights in the living room and the kitchen.

I can add more functionality using the infra-red capabilities, but until we get to that chapter, let's see what we can do with plugs.

Alexa Enabled Plugs

Plugs are possibly the best thing to use with Alexa. They not
only act as a switch that can be controlled using your voice,
but it can also report the status of the things that have been
switched on or off. In other words, it's a key benefit of smart
plugs to be able to work out whether something is turned on
or off. If Alexa is able to turn stuff on and off, it'd be much
better for Alexa to know that that thing turned on or off
successfully. You'd think that was a given, but sadly not.
With some smart stuff, you may not be able to get the status
of things. In particular, the infra-red on and off switches don't
let you know if it's on or off - other than looking at the light,
obviously. But what if you're out of the room? Or even out of
the house? The answer to that boggle has to be that there
needs to be a status that Alexa can understand. Smart plugs
are the way to go.

I really like smart plugs because it allows you to plug in
anything to turn a dumb device into a smart one.
Let's look at a tv for example. By using a smart plug, you're
able to turn it on and off, but the problem with that is that
(depending on the model of TV), it might not turn on directly
and you may then need an infrared controller to switch it off
standby mode. You will also need to take into account warm-
up times. I cover that a bit more in the infrared chapter (to
follow) but for now just understand that smart plugs are
simply switches. They can act as both triggers (Inputs) and
outputs for and from routines, scenes and strings. Let's get
into the nitty gritty of what I mean by these terms later on,
but for now, it's worth trying to remember I mentioned it.

Alexa And Smart Switches

Smart switches can come in a number of different form factors. We have already discussed the smart plug, which works as described before by turning on and off. It's essentially a plug socket that has a button on it and this button works like a remote switch. It's this switch that (like other switches), Alexa can access.

The switches, just like the plugs of the last chapter can report their status and this is possibly the most useful part of it. I've not gone into too much detail about why I used the smart plug for my LED strip lighting, rather than relying on the Infra-red command (which DOES work), but let's talk about it here a little bit.

I like to watch movies and TV – I mean, who doesn't? But I like to watch it in a fairly dark room. Not pitch black, as my kids would like it, but fairly dim. This is why I bought the LED light strip. Now, I wanted to be able to switch from sitting in the living room to watching TV by using my voice. I thought a command like "Alexa, movie mode" might be quite nice. The problem was that by using infra-red, I'd need the light either to be on or off for this to happen. The good thing about using a smart switch rather than infra-red is that Alexa can set the on or off to whatever I want and be sure it's doing it right.

The problem with the infra-red command was that on and off were the same command, so I would say "Alexa, movie mode" and it'd turn the LED strip off if it was on and on only if it were off. Not helpful. By removing the on/off from the "scene", I could add it to the routine instead, allowing Alexa to send an "on" command. But if the switch was "on" anyway, it'd just ignore it and leave the switch on. If it were off, it'd turn it on first and then dim it, turn it orange, switch on the TV… all that Jazz.

So smart switches CAN be the kind of plug I've mentioned already, but they can be wall switches like you've already got in your house. Sure, these require a bit of re-wiring, so if you do replace them, for goodness sake, please be very careful… it can kill you if you get it wrong.

That said, most smart switches require a neutral wire to work. The Lightwave RF doesn't! The smart switches in the rest of this chapter refer to the kinds of clicky buttons one has mounted to the wall of one's house. Now, what's groovy about these is that it overcomes the issue I just said in the "lights" chapter about your spouse turning off the light switch and you having to shout at Alexa until you realise the problem. Using a smart switch, you can have dumb and even dimmable dumb bulbs in your house. Your partner can flick off the light switch and you can simply say "Alexa turn the light on" and it'll come on again! Then you can have a game of "lighty lighty turny onny", and have hours of fun.

Or not...

The smart switches aren't cheap and require a lot more work than smart bulbs or smart plugs, but in my humble opinion are the best option, if you have the money and the time to install them. If you're not happy with swapping over the wiring, then get a professional to do it, but it's not too hard to do yourself. Just be sure you know what you're doing and are confident doing it. I don't want anyone trying to sue me for being a bit dead.

Alexa Enabled Thermostats

Ah, yes! Thermostats! Now this is a very clever little sensor and obviously I'm going to go into much more detail in the "sensors" chapter, but for now let me talk a bit about thermostats.

I've got the Nest 3rd generation learning thermostat and I love it. Linking all this stuff together using IFTTT and Stringify is certainly the best way to do this, but my thermostat is also a humidity sensor, so I'd be able (if I had one) to turn on the dehumidifier if it got too humid in my house. I can obviously do all the things you'd expect with a smart thermostat, like controlling the heating in my house wherever I am in the world. I can see on my phone what's going on in my house (heating-wise) but… and here's something cool you might not know… my thermostat has a proximity sensor.

I can link this proximity sensor with Alexa to give me a notification when someone moves within my house. This is potentially very useful when linked to my security camera and geo-location on my phone (more on this later).

I can set my heating to dip at night (most doctors recommend a temperature of around 16 degrees celcius at night) and let me tell you, it's improved my sleep dramatically. It's fairly easy to install (thanks to my friend, Mark for telling me how to do it), but if you're not confident, Nest can send someone around to your house for only £60, to install it for you!

What I like about the thermostat I have is that I can set a lock so the kids can't mess with my set temperature. Thermostats come into their own when you have more things to control the environment like watering plants when the temperature rises or turn on the dehumidifier when it gets too humid, turns off the heating when you turn on the air-conditioning and vice-versa. If you read the "sensors" chapter, you'll see more inputs you can use, but one example might be to use a window or door sensor to turn off the heating when there's a gaping great hole in your house. Thermostats have the potential to save your household / family money, but it depends on how smart you are and what else you can link to it.

Sensors For Alexa

Sensors come in all shapes and sizes and can (pretty much) do whatever you can think of.

If you want to measure the temperature, we've already discussed thermostats, but we can also buy extra thermometers that lack some of the thermostat's functionality. They're much cheaper than the hundreds you might pay for the nest thermostat but you won't be able to control your boiler (at least not directly), with it.

There are water sensors that you can put in-line to control whether you turn on and off water feeds to water the plants, run and stop pouring your bath, draw a sink full of water to do the dishes or even top up your swimming pool.
There are light and motion sensors that can detect movement, determine if someone is home or feed a dog when they go past a light beam.

There are door and window sensors that report when a window or door is opened.
We call sensors "triggers". These are part of the "if this happens" side of the IFTTT that I will cover in a later chapter. The sensors for part of the condition of your house and lets you have a deeper understanding of what's going on. We have already said about daisy-chaining these sensors to only turn on the heating of it's a certain temperature and the doors and windows are closed. You can automatically reject commands if the doors and windows are open and you can then get Alexa to tell you that your being stupid and wasting money.

Sensors can be anything from proximity sensors to heat sensors. Carbon monoxide sensors can tell you to get out of the house. Daylight sensors can trigger an alarm to go off in the chicken coup to wake up the cockerel, if you fancy a bit of revenge.

If you really start feeling a bit fruity, you can even use radar and echo location together with an arduino board to create a very sophisticated sensor. There's fingerprint recognition sensors, touchscreen inputs and keypads. There are buttons you can program to do specific actions and sliders that control anything from the lights brightness to curtains being drawn, music volume or anything else you want to happen. The limits are entirely of your own making.

Alexa And Infrared

Finally, we reach the dizzy heights of infrared. There are most likely many things in your house that use infrared rather than WiFi. These are most likely dumb things like DVD players or TVs. Be aware that even Smart TVs can be dumb when it comes to connectivity with Alexa.

We have already discussed smart switches and plugs to turn things on and off and even touched on the idea of a TV turning on using a smart switch, only to need breaking out of the standby mode using an infrared signal. Is there a way to do that using Alexa? Yes. Yes there is. It's not too hard either (thankfully). It works by providing Alexa with the capability of firing the infrared signal.

The problem comes when you look at the specifications of your devices and realise that most Alexa devices don't have the ability to fire infrared signals to other stuff. Most of the time (and all the things we have discussed so-far) work on WiFi. If your DVD player or Virgin Media box, sky TV or cable box doesn't have WiFi switching capabilities, you're screwed. And that's just for basic "on/off" stuff. What if you wanted to do more complex stuff? What if you wanted to change the channel? What if you wanted to record a TV programme, but the only way of doing it is using infrared? How would you go about doing that?

The answer is to use an infrared (IR) blaster. IR blasters work in a similar way to most Alexa devices in that they need an app for you to be able to program the device to work properly.

There are plenty of infrared plasters on the market that work with Alexa. The harmony hub, Beoadlink RM Pro and the cheaper Broadlink RM3 Mini are great options to use. I have to warn you though, in my experience the Broadlink customer service is useless, the software is unreliable and the skill is buggy as hell. After a LOT of pushing (around 6 weeks of talking to Amazon and Broadlink), I finally deleted everything from my app and started again and only then did it link to Alexa successfully. Having said that, my Broadlink RM Pro now works wonderfully and I'm very very happy with it. Would I recommend them? No, to be honest I wouldn't. I would say that if you follow all the instructions like I did, there's STILL no guarantee you'll get it working first time and t can be very very frustrating.

Let's assume you do get it working, however. What's great about it is the scenes it allows you to set up. I go into this in more detail in the scenes chapter, but for now understand that there are certain things that all linked together under a general umbrella. Scenes allow you to group together certain actions (like turning on the lights and the TV at the same time) all under one command. You might for example say "Alexa, let's watch a movie" and it'll turn on a scene for you that switches on the TV, lights and changes the temperature. Or you might say "turn on my movie scene" and it lowers the projector screen, turns on the projector and turns off the lights. The limitations are almost endless.

With my IR blaster, I can add multiple devices in the app that show in my Alexa device list as different devices. Although my TV, Apple TV, light strip and Virgin media set top box are all different devices, Alexa only ever sends signals to the Broadlink IR blaster. While we know it's sending commands to the IR blaster (and only that one device), each set of commands shows as a different device for the sake of the Alexa app. This is a handy little fiction because if we were to express what it's actually doing, it'd just say "tell the IR blaster to tell the TV to do X" and it'd be harder to differentiate the different signals for each device.

As it is, you'd be able to say "Alexa, TV on" and it's know that the TV device is not actually a TV. It's an IR device that controls the TV.

If you can imagine another person sat in your living room and you say "turn on the tv, please,' that person would not get up and press something on the TV. They'd press something on the remote control that would send the IR signal to turn the TV on. Same thing with Alexa. It's just asking the IR blaster to act like this imaginary human.

Infrared blasters allow you to control any device that works using infrared by storing the IR code in your account and linking that code to a function (like "turn living room red"). The most powerful aspect of this is when you use this kind of functionality to create scenes. So let's have little chat about what they are.

Alexa Scenes

Scenes are really powerful.

Imagine being able to control multiple things with a single command. Now, don't get me wrong, you can do some of this with routines and we'll get to that in a minute, but for now we need to know about how to use scenes.

A scene is a bit like a scene in a movie. Lots of things are going on in the same location. So lights might go on, temperature might go up or down, lights might change colour.

An example of a scene I created was a scene I called "movie night". With the command "Alexa, Open movie night", my lamp goes off, my light strip goes on, the light strip dims, the tv comes on, the light strip turns to a burnt orange colour, the Virgin Media set top box can also turn on, open my shows, adjust the volume on the telly… basically anything a human can do, my automation hardware can do using Alexa.

In another example, I might say "Alexa, intruder alert" and the light strip turns on, turns green and the main lamp uplighter in the corner goes off. Then Alexa says "what are you doing in my swamp" before playing a song from the movie, Shrek.

We have lots of little scenes like the ones above that allow us to control our home and they become even more powerful when you link them with IFTTT, so let's talk about that next.

<u>IFTT</u> – <u>What Is It And Does It Work With Alexa?</u>

IFTTT stands for If This, Then That. It's a kind of cloud based programming… ummm… thing. In other words, it's a service that is hosted online by another company. It allows you to link stuff together. It looks for when something changes. That's call the "If this" part and it "listens" for when something happens. That could be any of the triggers like you posting to Facebook or you get a tweet or the weather is getting hotter or your commute to work is looking busy. Lots and lots of triggers here from hundreds of services.

Then comes the "then that" part of the equation. This part is the action bit and it allows you to do any of the hundreds of actions that you can do on the hundreds of devices.

So you may want to turn your living room a certain colour or even send you a message, post to facebook, adjust the thermostat, water the garden, open the blinds and so on.

IFTTT can link with Alexa to give you more control over things using their service and it is a lot easier to use than routines and it can link to much more like Google Calendar and things like that. Yes, it can work with Alexa, but it's not limited. It's included here for what it can do with Alexa, but it's a tool that goes far beyond as well.

Using IFTTT, you can do things like making your lights flash red when you get a YouTube subscriber, email you a warning when your commute to work is too busy and the limit is your imagination.

But wait…

There is one more limitation. IFTTT is excellent but it does mean only one thing. The problem with it is that it doesn't really allow you to link more than one action or even more than one condition.

Recently, I had the need to inform my wife when I left work so that she knew I was on my way to pick her up but I knew I'd forget to let her know so I set up a routine in IFTTT.

The problem was that it fired at lunchtime when I popped out to pick up a donut from the shop. Needless to say my diet was ruined and so was the pretence that I was sticking to it. The answer was to find a service that would allow me to link multiple conditions and so along Came Stringify.

<u>Stringify</u> – <u>What Is It and How Does it Work With Alexa?</u>

Now that we have seen how awesome IFTTT can be (and it really can be), wouldn't it be great if it could do more? Well, yes. Along comes Stringify. There's a lot of talk on the Internet at the moment about Stringify becoming a threat to IFTTT and initially, I thought hat too, but they actually do different things.

IFTTT is something called a basic decision engine. In other words it does one thing based on one other thing. Quite literally, if this then that.

Stringify is different to IFTTT. It allows the user to generate strings of conditions so that some or all of them are true and do actions based off that.

Stringify has all the basics of IFTTT and - sure - you can use Stringify like IFTTT, but that (in my opinion) would be a massive waste of the enormous power of Stringify. Stringify allows you to make conditions like this:

<u>If</u>
I'm at work
And it's after 3 pm
And I'm going to leave
IFTTT can't do that kind of condition.

The other cool thing that Stringify can do that IFTTT can't is to string together the actions too. For example I have the following string:

<u>If</u>
I'm at work
and it's after 3 pm on a weekday
and I'm leaving
<u>Then</u>

Work out what the traffic is like
Work out the distance to my house
Work out the time taken to get home
Work out how long my house will take to warm up to the
correct temperature
Set my nest thermostat (based on how long it'll take to warm
the house)
Message my wife to let her know I'm leaving.

The reason the multiple conditions are needed is because I don't want to message her when I'm going on my lunchtime walk or visiting friends around there or going to the hospital or… whatever. It needs to be smarter than just IFTTT and so it is.

The other thing that I really love about Stringify is that it links not only to Alexa (for the Triggers), but also to IFTTT. So it's not really a competitor in my mind. It's more of an extension. So a simple flow I created in Stringify uses Alexa as an input to control a text message output and a notification on my iPhone. This uses IFTT too so it looks like this:

- IFTTT asks if I say a specific phrase in Alexa, then run the Stringify flow.
- The flow then says Message a specific number with a specific message and give me a notification.

It's a basic flow, but it gets around how to send a text message from Alexa for free and it helps to illustrate this point.

Routines

I just LOVE routines. They're a bit like Stringify and you can do things with Stringify that you can do with routines but unlike Stringify, routines work directly in the Alexa app and can also control Alexa outputs as well as inputs.

Routines in Alexa allow you to trigger stuff to happen at specific times, for example, some of my routines look a bit like this:

- At 5:20, all of the echo devices in the house (and we have about 9) start reminding us to take a regular medication.
- We have a wake up routine that starts the heater half an hour before we get up.
- We have a wake up alarm for the weekdays but not the weekends.
- We even have one set up that reminds my wife not to hog all of the bed!

There are routines that allow us to control multiple things at the same time too. So for example, our TV is a fairly cheap one and relies on infrared to change the channels and settings etc.

We can use a routine to turn it on, then using the Broadlink app, control a scene, then output some speech where Alexa says "okay, let's watch a movie", then a delay before the input is changed on the TV so we start watching Netflix or Apple TV or Virgin Media or a specific channel. Perhaps there's a delay before playing a song or turning something on, lowering a blind, turning on a projector… the limitations are non-existent. You can use these routines to do anything. I even made a joke one to tell my son that he stinks.

Alexa And Music

Yes, most Alexa devices (other than the echo input) do have speakers built in. The echo dot second generation and below sound like crap for most music playback so it's probably best to link a Bluetooth speaker or even hardwire it in. Music comes in multiple flavours with Alexa.

First, there's Spotify, probably the most comprehensive service on the market. It has podcasts that link to providers like anchor as well as all the major stations, providers, platforms, music makers and it's been around for ages so it's well established. Similarly, amazon music is obviously the preferred integration and that's what they try to push you towards for obvious reasons.

On the other end of the spectrum from these paid for services are things like TuneIn, a free service for people who like to listen to the radio. They have all the major stations but if you want a specific song, there's nothing quite like the paid for services, I'm afraid.

Linking It All together

All these features are cool on their own but it's when you link them all together that they become truly awe-inspiring. For example, every day at sunrise, you could program the sensor in the garden to turn on, measure the light and send it to IFTTT, which could then fire a camera to take a photograph of the sunrise, and upload it to Facebook, Twitter and even steam it live on you tube for a set period of time.

It could then send your phone a notification, send an email and message your mum (don't know why it should, but it could). You could then send an email out to your marketing list to say that the latest photograph of the sunrise is now online and for them to visit it.

In the meantime, using the same routine, you could be waking up to gently brightening lights as the sunlight levels get higher and higher and so in accordance with the rising sun, your smart blinds start to open and the coffee machine turns on to brew your morning drink. The music begins playing and over the top, you hear the latest news headlines and weather forecast.

All from a single routine and all without opening your eyes. It takes a while to set all this up, but it's entirely possible to do and once you've got it, the world will be a much nicer place to live in.

The Downsides Of Alexa

I'll admit, I've painted a pretty little picture of a world with Alexa in it. It's lots of shiny black plastic doing every one of your nasty little biddings but there may we'll be down sides. So what are they?

To be honest, it's sometimes hard to be objective but there may be some down sides we have not yet considered. Aside from the obvious time and money costs and the potential dangers of security, is there anything else we need to be aware of?

Sadly, yes.

When we use hubs that connect a whole load of stuff together, we need to pay for that hub.

Amazon are now insisting that certain services are held on the cloud rather than locally in the house of whoever owns the hardware. This can be seen as a good thing or… well… not.

If you've only one way of turning your lights on and off and that's using Alexa, you might want to think again. Don't get me wrong, I love Alexa and think it can really help you live your life far more efficiently but there are some downsides. Especially if you can't turn the lights on and off if the internet goes down. With hubs and devices taking up valuable WiFi slots on your WiFi routers, it's worth beating in mind that the more stuff you have the worse performance you will get on all of them regardless of what speed you're getting. It's a consideration and can help you to workout how many hubs you get.

If you're going down this route then do plenty of research and maybe join some You Tube channels about it.

Be aware of any down sides before investing your hard earned cash.

Most importantly of all, have fun with it. There are good things to come from all of this, but if you are aware of the risks, down sides and costs then perhaps you will feel free to just go for it and start making your life easier with Alexa.